The Year of Living Dangerously

A Survival Guide for Probationer Teachers

Diane Allison

·EDINBVRGH·

THE CITY OF EDINBURGH COUNCIL

EDUCATION

The following are trademarks and are recognised as such:
Coco Pops
Lemsip
Tipp-Ex
Blu-Tack
Bubble Wrap

First published in 2000 by
The City of Edinburgh Council
Education Department
Wellington Court
10 Waterloo Place
Edinburgh EH1 3EG

Reprinted February 2001
Reprinted July 2004

ISBN 1 902299 11 6

Contents

For my family who instilled in me a love of stories,
Stuart Robertson who inspired me to study literature,
and Ann Mortimer who taught me how to teach.

Introduction

Don't you just hate introductions? I've been sitting here trying to think of something profound to write for the last ten minutes, but it's a Tuesday, I've got a cold, I've just taught all morning on one cup of coffee and a bowl of Coco Pops, and I've got a 'please take' next period. So don't plan on being dazzled by my wit or brilliance just yet – I'm building up to it!

I was delighted to be asked to write this guide, although my emotions went something like this – elation–terror–anxiety–panic. (As with your first 'crit' lesson – the elation part being when the bell rang for the end of class!) I'm currently alternating between all four.

What you are about to read is principally a collection of my own thoughts, feelings and insights into my first year of probation, but I'm very grateful to friends and colleagues who have helped broaden the scope of this guide by offering their own opinions and experiences of Year One for your perusal. How wonderfully comforting it is to discover that other people can be just as inept as me when given the chance.

If you have absolutely no qualms at all about what's in store for you over the next few months, I'd recommend the complete works of Chekhov – this is not the book for you. This guide is for the rest of us who, amongst other things, find it difficult to build up flat packs, join the wrong queues at fast food outlets, and know the utter desolation of being greeted with the words 'This cash machine is not in service'.

My hope is that this book will serve as a sticking plaster, a comfort blanket, and a soother, as well as a practical help and guide for all you semi-ordinary people out there (I say 'semi' because you have, after all, chosen teaching as your profession). Okay, I've got to go – it is definitely time for more coffee.

Starting Off

Before You Start

Congratulations! If you are reading this then you've got a job and, whether that's one on a permanent full-time contract or a week's supply, you've made it over the first hurdle. Your thought bubble probably looks something like this:

'So now what do I do?... I've got a jo-ob!... What's the procedure?... I've got a jo-ob!... What did they say at college?... I've got a jo-ob!'

As many probationers are appointed in June or some time in the summer holidays, I'm going to write this section with the summer as a starting point and I'll leave you to adapt what I write here to fit in with your own calendar of events.

'Procedure' is a scary, forceful sounding word, so let's call this section 'Before you start, it would be an idea to ...'

Now that you know you have a job (yeehah!), try to visit the school you'll be working in at least once more before your start date. This should give you the opportunity to meet other colleagues and get to know the ones you'll be working most closely with a bit better. You can find out which room(s) you'll be in and what your timetable is likely to be (remember though, changes might be made before you start), and you can ask some of those burning questions that have been keeping you up at night.

If you don't already have one, ask for a copy of the School Development Plan (great for insomnia), the Department Development Plan (if you're in a secondary), the Department Handbook, and course syllabuses. It's worth familiarising yourself with policies on homework, assessment, discipline and, in the primary sector, the biggies – Language and Maths. There should be documentation on this – ask if you can have a copy. See if you can borrow single copies of any texts or units you are likely to be going to want to use with your class or classes. It's worthwhile finding out what the system is for booking out resources at this point, as the materials in your new school may bear little or no resemblance to the ones you grew comfortable with in your placement schools. It is wise to plough through a variety of these before you start, so take a suitcase in with you and fill it! (I exaggerate.) Actually, I did fill a suitcase with books once – it was when I was coming home after 'studying' for a semester abroad. It was like carrying a bag of bricks, so be careful with your back and do get permission before you empty the book cupboard.

Find out about other resources that are likely to be available to you, for instance listening boxes, overhead projectors, TVs, radios, videos, computers, and laptops. There will probably be a system for booking these – you need to know what it is. This is also a good time to sort out your college notes and any materials you've gathered, separating the good from the bad and the ugly.

If it's possible, try to arrange a chat with the previous teacher(s) of the class or classes you are about to take over. This will give you valuable insights into class dynamics: who to keep together, who to separate, who will need a lot of support, and who will – how can I put it? – need special firmness! Ultimately you need to make up your own mind about your pupils – one

teacher's little horror is, after all, another teacher's little gem –
but discussing your new class or classes with wiser, more
experienced colleagues is unbelievably helpful. Ask them if you
can see copies of your pupils' work, report cards and records.
The more information you have and the more time you have to
sift through and make sense of it, the better. You'll feel a lot
more confident.

There will be other documentation you'll want to have a look
at too, for instance, in many departments, teachers are expected
to fill in forward plans. These vary in detail from school to
school – it's good to know what will be expected of you. Ask
when assessment deadlines are, what you will be expected to
record, and how National Testing is organised (there is often a
pro forma system for this). The more you know, the easier it will
be to plan ahead.

If you're lucky enough to get one, you'll be dying to have a
good look at your new classroom. You'll want to find out when

you can move in, but be sensitive. I recently started a new school after a wonderful spell at Liberton High School. My classroom there was like my second home and it pained me to start moving all my things out, even though I was looking forward to a new start. I would have hated to feel rushed.

It's great if you can move in over the summer as you then have plenty of time to rearrange the furniture and move all your own stuff in. Check first though with the janitors that your room isn't scheduled to be used for anything over the hols, as you might walk in on your first day back and be horrified to see all your desks and chairs piled against the wall instead of where you so painstakingly positioned them. That's unlikely, but it's best to be in the know. It's also a good idea to make the janitors aware that you are actually moving in (!) – you'll probably need to get keys from them anyway and may need to sign in and out of the building.

Have a good look at all the furniture and equipment in your room before you start to move things about – you can take a peek at other classrooms along the corridor for inspiration. Obviously if you're a scientist, for example, there's a limit to what you can do to change the layout of a lab.

If you're in the primary sector, labelling things like group names, pegs, and trays will be an important task for you. You also need to think in terms of zoning (the location of your reading corner, maths area, choosing /activity area, and so on).

My advice is keep it simple and remember the basics. For instance, your pupils need to be able to see the board without getting a crick in their necks. They need to be able to access certain resources frequently, whilst other things can quite easily be tucked away and only brought out on the rare occasion when you're going to want to use them.

Think carefully about wall space and what needs to go up there. I love my *Romeo and Juliet* poster (the one with Leo and Claire) and I've collected loads of other great wall coverings, but what comes first has to be allocating space for displaying pupils' work.

Finally, before you leave, have a good look round the school and the grounds (if you can, take a drive around the catchment area too). This is a really good time to get your bearings, locating important facilities like the staff loos, the photocopier, staffroom, library, Learning Support base, medical room, and fire escapes.

Ideally, you'll get a tour of the building, but, if not, just ask if you can have a wander around. This will give you a deeper sense of belonging and you won't feel a fool getting lost on your first 'please take' / 'on call' / 'yuftie' two weeks into the first term.

Planning

As a student, your planning will have consisted of preparing for single lessons or, at most, a unit of work, so it's a strange feeling to all of a sudden be having to plan out whole terms for several classes or several aspects of the curriculum. It's hard knowing how much you should be covering. How long does it take to cover Unit One or this one particular novel?

My advice? Ask. Take the novel for example. In some schools you will only be given four to six weeks to cover certain major texts because they are always in demand. A famous example is *Of Mice and Men* – it's a great novel, accessible on many levels, so everyone wants it. In contrast, if you say you want to do Brecht with your fifth years, I doubt anyone will chase you up for his stuff – he's not exactly 'must read' material for teenagers – but that doesn't mean you can take all year to cover one of his plays. See what I'm saying? You really should ask colleagues who've been there, done that and bought the T-shirt what their approach is, and before you start making up worksheets like there's no tomorrow, ask what the department has – you may be pleasantly surprised to find that there's a whole pack of resources. It's so much easier and far less time-consuming to adapt something that already exists.

In many subjects, guidelines come with the materials you will be using, telling you how many hours or weeks it will take to get through the work you will be covering. And then there are assessment deadlines. Using these in conjunction with the syllabus or unit notes gives you a pretty good idea of how long you have to get through that particular segment of the course.

Differentiation is crucial, so the more you know about the class or classes you will be taking over the better. What levels or grades are they currently working at? Do any of your pupils have an auxiliary working with them? Who receives regular Learning Support? Do any of your kids use a laptop or a spell-checker? Once again, ask! If the answer is yes to any of the above, seek advice on how to proceed. Nowadays more and more pupils seem to be on IEPs (Independent Education Programmes) which means you will be expected to tailor your lessons carefully to meet their particular needs. But you shouldn't be expected to do this on your own. Often the Learning Support department will help you adapt materials – in some schools they will actually provide you with some materials. Cool! Find out what is expected of you as this will give you a head start and help you feel more secure.

Remember a couple of things here: firstly, there are many ways to differentiate, and, secondly, you are not superhuman – no matter what you said at the interview – and neither are your colleagues. Lots of good ideas are built into the guidelines you'll be using, for example the Programmes of Study in 5–14. Try to be clear on what, how and when you plan to cover the different aspects of your subject(s), and always bear in mind that the process your pupils go through is as important as the content they will be exposed to. Pay attention to breadth and balance. It's tempting to focus on the things you feel comfortable with (or just like), but you need to ensure that your coverage of the curriculum is balanced and fair.

The summer holidays are a great place to start getting things ready – ploughing through the documentation, familiarising yourself with resources and pupils' work, arranging your classroom and making some forward plans. But don't go overboard – you probably won't even get half of that done and that's okay. It's really important to relax and enjoy these holidays. You are going to want to feel fresh and rejuvenated when you start your new job, so, in a way, chilling out is the most important preparation you can do.

The First Day – Staff Only

Sexist comment coming up: if you're a man, this section probably won't seem as important to you as it will to some of the women out there. I'll be brief.

Check beforehand what the usual first-day wardrobe is in your new school. Believe me, this could save you considerable embarrassment. I turned up in my best skirt and silk blouse and my friend Morna bought a pink suit for the occasion. We were both met by jeans- and trainers-clad colleagues. The only folk that looked dafter than us were the men in jade joggers and grey loafers with thick white terry-towelling socks – they'd obviously had a fashion bypass at some point.

Every school is different, but, in most schools, casual is the order of the day and since this is your very first first day, I'd advise smart (as opposed to scary!) casual.

Oh, and before leaving for work, go easy on the caffeine intake. You are about to be issued with masses of paper and forms of every shape and colour, you're going to be barraged with names, faces and information and your head will be buzzing – the last thing you need on top of that is an espresso flashback.

My how-to-handle-the-first-day advice? Don't try to take it all in – your head will explode and that's really no way to make a good impression. Put a box or tray on your desk and mark it 'pending'! Write down as much as you can, and aim to remember the names of your colleagues when you're introduced to them. Keep your programme handy so that you know what's coming up next. And the rest? Well, that can wait till you get home, collapse and then clear that tray!

I remember it so well. That first day I was totally mesmerised. It really hit me that this was the first day of my new career and these confident, strange, noisy adults were going to be my colleagues for better or for worse. Everyone congregated in the staffroom and all the conversations were the same – how short the holidays had seemed to be! There was an air of novelty and of expectancy too. Nobody looked stressed (astonishing) and some folk even seemed quite happy! A lot of people smiled at me, and one or two introduced themselves. I didn't want to appear pushy so I just went with the flow and tried to look approachable.

Be aware that in some staffrooms it is a capital offence to use someone's mug or milk or sit in 'their' chair. Remember how Jack Nicholson looked in *The Shining*? Well, unless you want someone to go psycho on you like that with axe in hand, I'd bring my own stuff and check before sitting down that it's okay to have that seat. After all, the idea is to live through the first year!

That said, you don't need to be a mouse. Many staffrooms have lockers; ask if you can have one. Then bring in your herbal tea bags or your emergency chocolate bars and invest in a nice new mug. Other useful locker items: a packet of mints, Lemsips, pain-killers, and some instant soup and health bars, for the days when you didn't have time or couldn't be bothered to make your lunch up.

When it comes to relationships with staff, try to avoid the clandestine variety (!) and resist the temptation to cling to your department like a limpet, sitting exclusively with them; but remember the importance of loyalty to your department who are, after all, your life support system. Get to know other members of staff, but avoid gossip. Politics within a school can be very complex so watch your step. You can remain neutral without being anonymous.

Try to bear in mind that there will still be a kind of holiday atmosphere. You don't want to spoil this by asking questions that can easily wait until your colleagues have got back into 'work mode'. And don't be put off by people asking you why on earth you've chosen such an awful profession – sometimes the staff members who seem the most cynical are actually marshmallow on the inside. First impressions aren't always right. Give your colleagues the chance you want them to give you, and always remember there's a story behind every off-the-cuff remark.

I think my first day started with a whole-staff meeting over coffee and scones. I can't for the life of me remember what was discussed, but I do remember having to stand up at one point for everyone to have a good look at me. In my new skirt and silk blouse. Nightmare!

After the staff meeting, we split into departments and spent some time getting all the jotters and stationery sorted out. Your school will have its own system for this, for example using different sized jotters for different aspects of the curriculum or different year groups.

This is a good time to ask what the jotter policy is for the pupils. Are they allowed to write in pen or does it have to be pencil? Do the jotters need to be covered? Is there an edit code? What are you supposed to do about spelling mistakes? And – here's the biggie – are the kids allowed to use Tipp-Ex?! As well as jotters, your kids may be given plastic or card folders or both (in English, for example, one is usually for class work and the other is for redrafted work – your department should have a policy on redrafting), but, as I say, all this varies from school to school, so (you've guessed it) you're just going to have to ask.

You should be issued with a couple of register books and a record book. I was also given pens, pencils, a stapler, chalk, paper clips, and so on. It was great! I was even given a week-to-view academic diary (after I'd just forked out for one at John Lewis) and a teacher's planner. This doesn't happen in every school, but it is worthwhile holding off buying your stationery until you see what your school provides. Primary teachers should be issued with scissors, paints, calculators, rulers, and so on as well. A fly swat is a great investment (wasps will track you down!), but remember you only get a fortnight's wages at the end of your first August on the job, so don't get carried away!

If you're a primary teacher, this is a good day to find out where the kids line up, put their coats, and keep their bags and lunch boxes. If the front door has an alarm, find out what the number is. And while we're on numbers, ask about the photocopier code – not to be confused with your cash-card number! Oh, the stories I could tell. I really think they should run in-services on how to fix paper jams, add toner and translate the 'Help!' instructions on these machines. And don't get me started on computers.

This next bit is the best bit of the day. At some point, if you have your own room, you'll be given a short time (it will feel like a very short time) to arrange your furniture (if you haven't already done so), put up your posters, find a place for your plant and decide where to store your jotters and folders. Make sure you use this time well. Look inside all the cupboards in your room. There may be stuff left over from the previous tenant, some worth saving, some for the bucket. Check! Sometimes text books or other resources need to be stored in the classrooms because there isn't enough room in the department cupboards. Ask what should be in your room; sometimes things just haven't been put back where they belong. You want to make that room feel yours before the onslaught.

If you don't have your own room, find out where you are supposed to store things. If you are going to be working in the same groups of classrooms on a regular basis, you should be offered a little cupboard and wall space. If nobody offers, ask your PT about it.

On your first day there will probably be some kind of programme which will usually include some in-service training in addition to department time and the whole-staff meeting. As a new teacher you should get a guided tour of the school and an in-depth look at your department. If you have any free time, go down to Learning Support, the library and Guidance to introduce yourself as the new kid on the block. If you can't do this on your first day, it's worthwhile asking the member of staff in charge of probationers to arrange this for you. It's also in your best interest to 'get in with' the janitors, cleaners, kitchen and office staff. They can make or break your career!

In some schools the first in-service day is also the time for booking texts. I ended up having to do *The Otterbury Incident* with my second years (hardback, old, very old, faded pink – have I said these books were old? And that I had never read the novel before and there was not a single resource on it?). So, I can tell you, you really want to get in there and book out something good.

I suppose the first day alternates between being stressful, exciting and surreal, because everything is so new. You are trying not to look out of your depth and you want to make a good impression, and this raises the stress factor – as well as your acting skills – considerably. Don't worry though. You don't have to ask all your questions on the first day and you certainly don't have to understand everything. Just remember – breathe, smile and try not to look too gormless.

The Real First Day – Meeting the Kids

At the Secondary

The first group of pupils you are likely to meet is your register / form / tutor class. Hope for first years – they won't know you're new! Before the kids arrive, you'll probably be issued with their timetable and blank timetables for them to fill in. This sounds simple, but, if you are really creative, you should still manage to get in a kerfuffle. I do, every year, despite being given all the information I need and a kind of idiot's guide to timetabling. What can I say? I'm special.

In some schools a meeting is arranged for new register teachers on the first in-service day. This sorts things out for most people and makes the next day straightforward, but for those of us who like to live on the edge some things will still be as clear as mud after the briefing. Don't worry – somehow it all works out fine in the end.

It's tempting to get bogged down with all the paperwork on that first meeting with the kids. You usually have to distribute lots of bits of paper like the school rules and the calendar. Don't linger on all this stuff – you can reinforce it all later. My advice is to use the time to get to know the kids. Registration is always extended on the first day (probably because some of us take longer than others over the timetabling bit!) so make the most of the time you have to break the ice.

Remember you are a first-level Guidance teacher, the first member of staff kids see each day, and you can build up a really rewarding relationship with them if you are willing to make the effort. Bear in mind too that this may be your register class for several years, and the chances are you will teach a number of these pupils as well over the years, so get to know them. Names are vital. It's up to you how you do this – some folk like playing games, others prefer a more one-to-one approach.

In general, registration lasts about ten minutes (except on the first day when it usually last about an hour). What the kids experience in those ten minutes is largely up to you. I am not a morning person; I like to ease myself into the day, so I have a lot of sympathy for the kids who come in with their eyes still shut. I'm quite happy to let them chat quietly for the first few minutes while I sort through the notices and speak to individuals about absences and the like. It is a good idea however to insist on silence while you actually take the register and read out the bulletin or any other notices. It's also a good idea to allocate a small piece of wall space to your register class for notices.

It sounds daft, I know, but find out what actually constitutes someone being late: in some schools if you appear for registration after the teacher has taken the register, you are marked down as late, even if the bell hasn't gone for the end of registration. Try to be consistent from the start and remember your dual role as administrator and Guidance teacher. You'll benefit from this as much as the kids – you find out more from them about what's happening in the school than from any staff bulletin!

It's a good idea to keep a note folder for your form class. Allocate each pupil a plastic wallet with their name on it and stick their notes and late slips inside, dating and signing them first. This is also a good place to store medical details and relevant family details (asthmatic; big sister in S4 carries spare inhaler; grandfather in hospital). This turns into a pretty good Guidance file after a few months and can be really useful.

You will probably be in close contact with Guidance staff concerning the pupils in your register class (they may expect you to send out absence enquiries), so the more you know about your kids, the better. Be aware that, as a register teacher, you may be asked or expected to become involved in programmes such as the buddy scheme (where older pupils come into your form class, and are involved in various activities with the younger kids to help them settle in) or target-setting (a number of schools now have designated senior teachers who are responsible for working with particular year groups or pupils to help raise attainment). The first time you meet each class is pretty much the same. You will be issued with class lists and asked to check off who is there against who should be there. (It doesn't happen very often, but sometimes kids deliberately opt to go to the wrong class, in the hope that no one will notice and they can stick with their pals or a teacher they are particularly fond of!) Take a note of each pupil's register class, teacher and room as well as their practical set, as this makes it easier to track kids down and you need some of this information for report cards. After this, you will probably want to issue jotters and other materials relevant to your subject area and establish where they will be kept. For S1 in particular, you will have to explain what jotters and folders are to be used for: rough work, best work, or whatever.

This is a good time to discuss:
- what you expect of your class and what they can expect of you (code of conduct)
- what the course for this particular year group will consist of
- the correction code
- jotter policy, homework policy, and borrowing policy
- consequences and rewards.

How you handle your first classes will have a lot to do with your personality and style. I try to make the first lessons interesting and fun while at the same time being really firm with those who do not wish to cooperate. Remember, the pupils' perceptions of you will be formed largely in this period so try to establish routines and boundaries from the beginning – it's hard (though not impossible!) to reinvent yourself later. You may feel uptight, but try not to act it! If you appear confident and relaxed and seem to be enjoying yourself, this will go a long way towards creating an environment where your pupils feel secure and motivated. Go for it!

At the Primary

Because primary pupils spend most of their school day in the same room with the same teacher, it is crucial that routines are established as quickly as possible. The first order of the day is to establish a classroom code of conduct. This is often done in discussion with pupils, phrasing rules positively and making the pupils feel involved in the process. Rules should be clearly displayed on the wall, but also need to be explained and illustrated, particularly for younger children.

The first day is also a good day to go over the fire drill and show the class where everything is kept – the finished work tray, the bin, paper, colouring pencils, rulers, and so on. Your pupils also need to be clear on where they keep their own stuff like lunch boxes, bags and coats.

Work out a clear system for your administrative duties such as dealing with dinner money, the register, late slips, trip money, and medication. Ask how other colleagues manage this. It is vital that you stay on top of all this from the start, recording everything clearly. (Don't ask about me, the pantomime, the spreadsheets and the tickets – I wasn't trying, but I nevertheless managed to define 'chaos'! Check your dictionary – I'm right there beside 'pandemonium', 'mayhem,' and 'shambles'.)

If you haven't already been told, it's important to find out about the health of your kids. Do any suffer from allergies or epilepsy or asthma? Who is on medication and what is the procedure for this? Also find out if there are any pupils you really need to watch out for in terms of discipline. Forewarned is forearmed!

Getting Through the Year

The First Weeks

You need to do some diagnostic assessment at the start to find out for yourself what the needs of each of your pupils are – you may need to meet with Learning Support colleagues to discuss this. You're also going to have a lot of reading to do in your first couple of weeks – stuff like primary reports, the third-year folders of your fourth-years or the P5 folders of your P6 class, and reports passed on from colleagues about individual pupils in your classes.

In your first week find out who had Learning Support the previous year and for what, and check that you have all the relevant info about your kids – who has hearing or visual impairments, and so on. By rights, some of this information should have come to you already from Guidance, LSS, or a previous teacher, but these are busy people with priorities of their own, so be polite and patient!

Establish a good, hard-working atmosphere early on and be organised about homework. Check policy – some departments issue homework jotters and some schools do not allow homework to be issued unless pupils are going to be given a full week to complete it.

Try to start issuing homework from the first week (it should be part of your planning when making up units of work), so that your pupils get used to having homework from your particular subject. Other departments/colleagues will be doing this and, if you leave it for a few weeks, the pattern will be set before you can become a part of it; typical comments from your pupils will be, 'You can't give us homework tonight – we always get French and Science homework on a Tuesday'. Of course you can give homework any time you like, but you want to be perceived as an organised teacher who gives homework regularly. This is especially important with exam classes, where to a great extent the kids rely on you to set the pace. You want to make sure that your subject isn't perceived as a soft option. At the same time, be inventive – you can make homework fun as well as challenging. It doesn't always have to be written work, it could be research or interviewing someone at home, or bringing something into class. Watch this last one though – unless of course you're happy to have an iguana or a stick insect zooming around your classroom on 'show and tell' day. (If all else fails, remember the fly swat!)

Remember too that, on the whole, written homework has to be marked by you, so it's a good idea to stagger the days on which you issue and collect it from your various classes. Keep a clear log of dates set and who has done what. In some schools you'll be expected to send letters home informing parents when their children are not keeping up-to-date with homework, or are presenting work of poor quality, but I also think it's a good idea to actively reward those who always do their homework well. I sometimes use merit points and give a prize to the pupil with the most points at the end of each term.

If you're a primary teacher, find out whether your pupils

should start working in their jotters straight away, or whether paper should be used in the first few weeks. And, August or not, there's something else you want to find out quite quickly – the wet weather policy!

The first couple of weeks are a good time to set targets, especially with senior pupils so that they have a clear agenda to work to. This is a good time to give your classes an indication of where they will be headed over the next few weeks. Quickly establish a routine – pupils feel secure when they are clear about what they are doing and what exactly is expected of them.

In the first week or two your classes may either be a complete nightmare – always playing up, stretching your patience, trying to see how far they can go – or they may be quite well-behaved; it depends on their strategy! If they are well-behaved, don't be lulled into a false sense of security – they are sussing you out, and soon enough they will try things on with you to see how far they can go. If they are a complete nightmare, don't despair –

once they get used to you they will slacken off. They are simply testing the boundaries. Be aware of trouble zones, like those days when you teach back to back without a minute to yourself, or last thing on a Thursday afternoon when tempers can be a bit frayed!

The Next Few Months (Making it to Christmas)

I'm an autumn girl. I love the colours and the way the weather changes from warm, bright sunshine to freezing, face-numbing rain.

If you're a primary teacher, be ready to start preparing for all the Christmas activities as soon as you get back after the October break. Get your tinsel, glue and frieze ideas sorted out – try to keep it simple. Make sure you know exactly what's expected of you, and ask what other colleagues have done in the past.

You may have whole-school activities to get ready for – a nativity play or a show. The secret is to plan ahead, be flexible, and then enjoy the process of getting to know the kids better as you mix regular class work with these other activities.

If you're a secondary teacher, you may have to get your pupils ready for prelims. The same types of questions turn up nearly every year in the exams, and it's your job to make sure your pupils understand what these questions require them to do (and then have the necessary skills and subject knowledge to tackle them). Don't just expect exam classes to do one past paper after another in preparation. It's often a good idea to pick out key questions, or to split the class so that, for example, Group A tackle questions 1–5, Group B numbers 6–10, and so on. Be inventive. Let's face it, this time of preparation is not necessarily going to be the best fun you have with the kids all year, but neither does it have to be complete drudgery. Don't save all the fun for your junior classes – 15- and 16-year-olds enjoy treats too and often work harder after one. You should see me on a Friday morning after my treat – a still-warm cherry scone, they're soooo yummy.

November can be tough because it's caught between autumn and Christmas. It's what I call a 'not yet' month – not yet time to loosen up and not yet winter wonderland time. That's why I love getting into December. The kids are not the only ones who get excited about opening that first advent window! I just love the whole build-up to Christmas. The nights are long and dark, and the days are short; but, although you'll miss the sunlight, there's a buzz and the countdown's getting lower every day.

It's a wonderful feeling to get to the Christmas hols and realise that you've been teaching for nearly half a year. You've left the base camp far below and scaled the heights. You've still got a long way to go, but the important thing is that now you know you can climb.

From January to March (Making it to Easter)

The Christmas holidays fly by and, before you know it, it's January, you're broke and the weather matches your mood – bleak. Over the next few weeks you will see colleagues dropping like flies with assorted ailments: flu, chest infections and various 'itises'. So now is the time to do the following:
- work out a savings plan (again)
- wear those woollies you got for Christmas
- invest in some multivitamins and eat lots of fresh fruit and veg
- make sure you get enough sleep, and then some
- buy some travel brochures – at least you can look at all those sun-soaked tropical shores!

This next bit is mainly secondary-orientated. Forgive me – as an English teacher, I need to get this out of my system. My analyst says it's good for me!

Term Two in the secondary school just doesn't feel long enough, and yet, in other ways, it's groundhog term. Sometimes it seems that spring will never arrive. The main pressure is that all your exam classes' folios, investigations, projects, and dissertations must be completed before the end of this term. These pieces should be an integral part of your planning, but now you'll be focusing on them a lot more than on other classwork. You must get into this at the very beginning of the term. You'll already have some work under your belt from the first term, but, believe me, you'll wish you had more! You will not be the only teacher to hyperventilate, scream, or pass out when you look in certain kids' folders, but don't despair – there is still time.

This is the make or break term for your Standard Grade and Higher / Higher Still classes. Set targets, both for them and for you, and try to ensure that your pupils take responsibility for their own progress. Responsibility is actually an important issue from S1 right through to S6. If your first-years are trained in independent learning and aren't spoon-fed, they will make far better senior pupils, because you will have trained them to be self-motivated. Don't forget they've had seven years of primary education where this training began.

It's important to remember that you are not the only one feeling the pressure this session, although it may sometimes feel this way. Your pupils have pressing commitments in other subjects, and assignments for all of these have to be handed in at roughly the same time (usually mid-March to mid-April.) Some pupils will attempt to transfer their pressure on to you and make you feel totally responsible for their work. You have to put the ball back in their court and make them take responsibility for it. In the end, their commitment, or lack of it, will go a long way in determining what marks they get. Finally, make sure that the kids know that a deadline is a deadline.

The one good thing about Term Two is that homework which was sluggish in coming in during Term One will mysteriously start to appear. You'll find your break times and lunch-times will disappear as interested, nervous, conscientious, overwrought, or confused pupils all crowd into your room to glean nuggets of wisdom!

SHOCK – EXTRA homework will be requested.

HORROR – ALL marking will be expected back immediately.

Internal assessment is the other biggie in the second term for a number of subjects like Talk in English, orals in Modern Languages, and practicals in Home Economics and Science. For fifth- and sixth-year pupils involved in Higher Still courses, internal assessments will be spread throughout the year (although many of them may fall in this term), and your PT should give you dates for these so that you can plan your course around them. Check the department policy on arranging resits and discuss the documentation, such as record sheets and evidence, that you'll be expected to keep for each of your Higher Still classes.

There are no two ways about it: Term Two is exhausting. It is a daunting task to prepare your first senior classes for their exams. The good thing is that, finally, even your laziest kids will experience a rush of motivation, will actually listen to your advice and, in some cases, will hang on your every word! Just let the adrenalin work its magic, and hang in there. Then you can collapse in a heap at Easter.

From April to June (Making it to the Summer Holidays)

If you make it to the summer term in one piece, you have really made it through your first year, as the third term is, in many ways, easier than the first two. Not only have you forged a place for yourself in the school, got to know staff quite well, got a grip on your classroom management skills, and built up a comforting pile of resources, you'll also have got to know your pupils inside out and become really attached to some of them (!), not to mention living through the Christmas show and all manner of folios, projects, investigations, and assessments. You've got most of your act together, you know you can do it, you like doing it and you want to keep doing it!

At the Secondary

Alas! You'll only have your S4, 5 and 6 classes for about two weeks before their exams start and they go on leave. You really need to get the max out of this short time. Exam practice is the order of the day, but remember that there are loads of ways of going about this and, as with normal lessons, you should vary your approach in keeping with the needs of your pupils (by this stage in the school year, you'll know exactly what they need).

Once the exams are on, you will be involved in a variety of other activities, but, if possible, try to catch your pupils on the way out of their exam to find out how they got on. They really appreciate this.

Exam leave is a great opportunity to try to get some of those things done that you've been meaning to do all year, but never got around to. You know: filing, cleaning out your desk drawers, filing, forward planning, filing, reading new texts, filing – and so it goes on to infinity and beyond! Don't be too ambitious about what you'll be able to get through – the time will just vanish, swallowed up by cover classes, meetings, report cards and looking at the beautiful big chestnut tree outside your window (or maybe that's just me!). Still, there's very little to be stressed about over this period and you do have more time to think, to take stock, and to make plans for the start of the new timetable. Carpe diem!

If the timetable in your school changes before the holidays, you will have to repeat the whole process you went through in August. There should be a policy for transferring information from one teacher to the next as you swap classes – make sure you know what's required well before the transfer date.

It can be a nightmare around this time: your energy levels will be quite low even though (or perhaps because) the holidays are in sight. This is the time when you can ask in the staffroom how long it is until the last day of term and at least three people will answer in unison, right down to the minute! That's when you know you're nearly there and you just have to hang in there a little longer.

Be aware that you lose kids to things like school concert rehearsals, field trips, career interviews, and early holidays in the third term. You have to have a Plan A and a Plan B where your lessons are concerned. Bear in mind too that the kids are getting into holiday mode. The ones who have just had exams will not be in the mood for anything too heavy and their attendance may leave much to be desired. Younger kids will be restless and your classroom will be too hot, even with all the windows open. This is the time to give the kids lots of easy, no-hassle, fun activities to hold their interest and keep you sane.

Try to do something fun for yourself in the third term. There are lots of extra things happening like concerts, fêtes, book weeks, prize-givings, and sports finals. Although you'll be tired, you'll also feel a great sense of achievement that you have got to this point in your career without losing your mind entirely. You can pat yourself on the back over a lot of things. You are known in the school and that makes such a difference; kids you don't even know will say hello to you as they pass you in the corridor; staff will now treat you as an equal, not a visitor, and you will have sussed so much out – the best time to get peace at the photocopier, how to get the janitor to find you those extra boxes you need, or the office staff that extra Blu-Tack.

You'll know what day chicken curry is being served at dinners, and you'll know the best place to go for a pub lunch. As you walk along the corridor to your classroom, it will just hit you one day that you belong, you have arrived, and it is good.

At the Primary

June is often a busy month in primaries. There's the sports day and an assortment of trips may be arranged. These range from visits to the zoo to famous historic landmarks. (Wherever you go, the kids will no doubt tell you that the highlight was stopping at the 'drive thru' on the way home!) Do be careful if you're involved in taking in the money for any of these excursions. Unless you want to start defining chaos yourself, my advice is never to think you'll remember – write everything down and bank all money daily. If you're helping with the sports day, try to make it fun for all the kids, some of whom would rather have a tooth pulled than take part in anything competitive or athletic. Self-esteem is an important issue, and all your pupils need to feel valued, not just the 'sporty' ones.

Your First Classroom

Even if it is the size of a cupboard, the walls are crumbling, and the paint peeling, it will still feel great to have your own room, and you'll love it! (Perhaps in the same way that mothers think their newborn babies are beautiful when, let's be honest, they often look like shrivelled prunes to the casual onlooker.)

Try to make your room a stimulating and welcoming environment. You will be spending several hours a day in it, so you have to make it feel yours. Grovelling to janitors and showing due respect to cleaners can work wonders. Remember, the janitor knows about surplus furniture. Cleaners will be very grateful if you get pupils to put chairs up at the end of the day and to put any litter in the bin.

It can be a good idea to involve the pupils in decorating your room (it is their room too and they have to create in it!), putting up posters, displaying their own work, watering plants, and so on. Bear in mind that in the case of many first-years this has been part of their primary school experience, and that kids are far less likely to make a mess of something they have put a lot of effort into themselves.

Resources

Accommodation and conditions vary tremendously, even within a school or an individual department. You cannot take resources like TVs, videos and computers for granted. (You can't take being able to operate them for granted either, but that's another story. Suffice to say I must have a lot of psychokinetic energy, because anything mechanical has the tendency to malfunction as soon as I go near it.) You should, at the very least, have a board and chalk, and some tables and chairs.

At college you may well have had enough free time to track down the resources you needed for the lessons you took on placement (especially for the dreaded 'crit' lessons). Indeed, students are actively encouraged to use equipment like overhead projectors, video cameras, and listening boxes – and all in the same lesson! As a first-year probationer, though, you simply won't have time to locate and use all of these resources for every lesson and, to be honest, you won't want to, since they won't be appropriate or necessary.

What tends to happen is that you'll plan ahead for using this kind of equipment, maybe once or twice a week, and that way you'll have time to set these items up and return them to their proper places without blowing a gasket or hogging all the equipment. Your pupils will still get the variety they need, while you become adept at using resources in a manageable way. You'll suss out loads of technical stuff too, like switching things off at the mains to clear errors!

In the primary it's important to find out about hall times, library times, TV room times and the timetables of visiting specialists. In some secondary schools you can also book the computing suite, library and LSS facilities at certain times of year.

Classroom Layout and Gender Issues

My granny died recently and is sorely missed by all who knew her. One of the things I love most about her was the way that she was always rearranging the furniture, particularly in her living room. You could go down to the baker's to get her a pie and, by the time you got back, the couch would be against a different wall and there would be a different coffee table and rug in the middle of the room. She taught me many things, and one of them is that there are no limits to what you can do with a little bit of floor space.

Here are some pointers that are worth bearing in mind when arranging the furniture in your classroom. First of all, if your room has no carpets then the scraping of desks and chairs can be very noisy. You need to think about the teachers in the surrounding rooms, which means that if you do decide to rearrange the furniture you should try to do this first thing in the morning, at break, at lunch-time, or at least when you have a group of sensible pupils with you, not a splinter group from your third year who are likely to start chucking chairs at one another. 'But Miss, it was just a toy fight, honest!'

That said, and while it is just not practical to change the layout of your room for every new lesson, it is nevertheless fun experimenting with different arrangements in the course of the year. Of course, it's not possible or even appropriate to do this in certain subjects.

If you're a teacher of a practical subject, you'll probably share a facility rather than have a room to yourself so you need to find out what the system is for storage and use of resources and what exactly the technician does. Like janitors, office staff and cleaners, technicians can make or break your career – so you be sweet.

I'm going to call this paragraph State the Obvious – you'll soon see why! As a student, you will have seen that certain seating arrangements work better for certain types of classroom activities and, as far as possible, you should try to match up the two on a regular basis: group work means group seating, paired work means sitting in pairs, tests usually mean sitting on your own, and so on. I can tell you're dazzled by my genius! Okay, nothing hard about that bit, but this next bit might take a little more thought.

If you want your pupils to work in groups, you need to be clear about the purpose of the group activity and what you would consider a successful outcome. First off, I would recommend groups of between four and six pupils, certainly never more than six – that would be a nightmare! My preferred number is five pupils per group, because the odd number means pupils are less likely to pair off or reach deadlock.

Most of the time I arrange the pupils into mixed-sex groups because such groups are usually more diverse, and I also think that it's important for boys and girls to learn to work together.

Remember, it's our job to facilitate personal and social development as well as teach our subject, and this is one very basic approach. At times, though, I do deliberately separate my pupils into single-sex groups – it all depends on the purpose of the task. Likewise, dividing pupils into ability groups for some activities and into friendship groups for others is also good practice – you just need to think clearly about what is going to be the best environment for effective learning with regard to this particular piece of the course. Also consider how you are going to ensure that each pupil remains engaged with the group activity for its duration. (Are there tokens to be spent? Does each child have a specific task?)

I know that some teachers fear and even frown upon group learning, but I genuinely believe that pupils have much to gain from consulting one another and working together; that purposeful talk and collaboration are actually great ways to learn. I think some teachers are afraid of losing control, but, from what I've seen, the serried-rank seating approach is no big stumbling block to those kids who are determined to have a blether about the latest teenage heart throb. It's easy to confuse classroom layout with classroom management, but they are two quite different things.

Probably my favourite seating arrangement is paired ranks (pupils sitting in twos, but not at random – more about that later). The reason why I love this is that, when I want my kids to work in groups, it is easy to turn chairs around so that they can work in groups of four without much hassle. From there it is easy to get them into fives or to rearrange the pupils without rearranging the furniture. On the other hand, when a test is arranged, it is easy to split the pairs into singles. The rest of the time they're either working with a partner or independently. But that's just me – you'll soon find out what you prefer. What's important is that you expose your pupils to a variety of groupings in the course of the year, in keeping with both the demands of the curriculum and their particular needs.

I always try to speak to the teachers of any classes I am taking over to find out about good and bad combinations of pupils and which pupils may need to sit near the front of the class because of hearing or visual difficulties. I then try to make sure that bad combinations are scattered to the four corners of the room – although sometimes it feels like there aren't enough corners to go round. Usually, my next step is to arrange my pupils so that they sit 'boy:girl', as I've found this to be very effective in terms of quality of learning and classroom management. I'll often position a very bright girl beside a boy with learning difficulties or vice versa, but bear in mind that this is not a permanent arrangement – both pupils will work in lots of other contexts as well. This is just one that I've found useful to start with.

It's a good idea to have one or two desks strategically placed so that disruptive pupils can be removed from their usual seats and isolated by the board, your desk or the door. Think as well about where you are going to position your own desk – it doesn't have to stay where you find it on the day you arrive.

It's also worth bearing in mind that, regardless of the groupings, boys and girls tend to learn in different ways because – shock – they think in different ways. (Suggested background research: *Men are from Mars, Women are from Venus* and most daytime television.) That means that if you rely too heavily on only one teaching and learning style, either the boys in your class or the girls may be at a disadvantage. Boys for example tend to respond better to measurable targets, as they tend to be more task-orientated. So, for a boy, 'Write down five pieces of information about Hawaii' is far more useful than 'Write a short paragraph about Hawaii'. In addition, you'll have noticed that boys tend to like active, hands-on lessons and work for praise whereas girls tend to be better organised, find it easier to give their work a structure, and tend to work for themselves. These are just some of the issues you need to consider when arranging your pupils and deciding on the best approach for your lessons.

The bottom line is that as long as you vary your approach in terms of layout and lesson style, you'll be fine and so will your kids. Don't be afraid to experiment, and take note of the lessons you learn along the way. Oh, and if you want to put a coffee table and a rug in the middle of the room, I say go for it!

Organising Your Time

Timetabling at the Secondary

Each school seems to have its own strange quirks when it comes to timetabling (actually, not just when it comes to timetabling – but that's not important right now!). Whatever your timetable, here are some things worth remembering:

- the timetabler didn't throw the curriculum in the air and decide on the new timetable according to how the pieces fell. Honest!
- there is a wider picture and it's usually pretty complex
- you probably couldn't do a better job yourself
- you'll adapt quickly to the hand you've been dealt
- it should be different next year.

In my school we have 35-minute periods, but most lessons are in doubles. We start at 8.45 and finish at 3.45 from Monday to Thursday. Fridays are different – the kids have a half day. In my last school, we started at 8.25 and break wasn't until 11.20. There were 40-minute periods, but that's just changed to 60 minutes. My point – and I do have one – is that you soon adjust to whatever the new routine is that you're going to be a part of, especially if you take my advice and swallow your timetable!

I always love getting my new timetable and I pore over it like it's a bestseller – sad I know. The first thing I look at is the times when I get each class. If I get class 3M on periods three and four on a Monday, periods one and two on a Wednesday, and period nine on a Thursday, the clear signal is that the bulk of the class work will be tackled on Mondays and Wednesdays, and that Thursdays' lessons will be simple and quiet because, by Thursday period nine, everyone is frazzled. I do that for all my classes.

Next, I look at my busiest day – there's always a day when you'll be stretched to the limits. If you're like me, you'll make that the day when your classes are finishing off work or redrafting, doing a lot of self-contained, non-hyper stuff. Then I look at the positioning of my non-contact periods (counting them carefully!) and I think about which single teaching periods would be good for library visits, homework checks, and so on.

I'm going to sound like Monica from *Friends* here, but it really is a good idea to make multiple copies of your timetable (keep one in your diary, one stuck to your desk, one at home, one in the staff base, and one in your handbag or briefcase). I know that sounds a bit excessive, but it's amazing how your mind can go blank or play tricks on you. I know someone who was sitting in the staffroom one day happily munching away at her lunch when a colleague came in with a grin on his face and asked her if she was having fun. Her second-years were rioting in the corridor – it was only 11 am! You think it'll never happen to you until it does.

As well as knowing your own timetable, it's a good idea to know what the rest of your department's is like. Apart from satisfying your curiosity, this can also help you out. For example, if colleagues are working in their room, but don't have a class, or have a particularly nice class, they may be willing to host a pupil who has misbehaved or who needs to catch up on a test. If you find that you are teaching the same type of class as a colleague, it's a good idea to chat to them about the tasks they set or the materials they use. This kind of discussion is invaluable, but do make sure it's a two-way street. I know that as a probationer you may feel that your ideas or your worksheets are dire and everyone else's are much better. However, you are the one who has been differentiating from the start, all your material is new and fresh, and any colleague worth their salt will appreciate your sharing with them as much as you appreciate their sharing with you.

As someone who was born on a Friday, perhaps it's only natural that it's my favourite day of the week. Not only are Fridays scone day, they're also divided up at my school so that, regardless of what's going on in the afternoon, you only teach in the morning. I really like that – it's a nice way to end the week.

Friday afternoons are still a bit of a mystery to me – a total X-File in fact. I've come to the conclusion that we're not actually meant to understand them – that's what your copy of the school calendar is for! Sometimes you'll have a department meeting and other times you'll have a whole-school or even neighbourhood meeting, and there are also afternoons where you get to go home.

Sometimes I do stay back on these free afternoons and get lots of work done, and that's great, but my advice is not to do that all the time. Other times I zoom out of the building like a rocket and head for the shops. I love meeting my mum and going for lunch, then wandering around. Retail therapy really does work wonders for me, but, if I'm skint, it's nice just to go home. In the wintertime, I can get into my jammies really early and watch a black and white movie as I snuggle up on the couch. In the summertime you can sit outside and read. It's your choice – just make sure that you enjoy yourself.

Non-contact Time

I always think this sounds like something out of a sci-fi novel, as if you have to walk around in a huge piece of Bubble Wrap and aren't allowed to touch, speak, or communicate in any way.

As I said earlier, one of the first things that most teachers do when they get their new timetables is look at how many non-contact periods they have and when they have them. The minimum time allocation is about 240 minutes a week, and, if you're on 'minimum', you shouldn't be asked to cover anyone else's classes (except during study leave when you have some slack on your timetable). If you have more free time than you're officially entitled to, expect to lose some of it each week covering absences. Every school has its own unique way of arranging this, and my advice is not to try to make sense of it – the system simply isn't compatible with human DNA.

I love all the jargon for teaching someone else's class. In some schools it's called 'cover', which makes me think of watching somebody's back in a gun fight or assuming a new identity. Then there's 'on call'; I like the medical connotations there – all that's missing is a beeper and a white coat (and any medical knowledge beyond what I've picked up watching *ER*). 'Please take' is another one – you don't need to be a genius to work that one out. It is slightly more pleasant than 'stand by' (which has country-and-western connotations). I think my all-time favourite though is 'yuftie' – short for 'Miss, yuftie take Mr Anderson's History class'. That one's definitely got something!

In most schools there's an 'on call' register so that you know exactly which periods you need to be available, and when you'll be free to go to the photocopier or get some reports written or whatever it is that you need to get done.

My advice for covering classes? Be prepared. (Sounds like I was a Guide, which I was, though not a very good one – how many girls do you know who failed their laundry badge? I did love the abseiling though – unrelated to aforementioned badge.) Never take anything for granted. Take paper and pencils, quiet-room slips, positive and negative referrals, and a couple of punishment exercises to boot. Also have some worksheets that the kids can make their way through if they finish early or if nothing has been left out for them in the first place. Usually the principal teacher of the department you'll be visiting will come along at the beginning of the lesson to make sure you have everything you need, and usually you do, but there are rare occasions when you'll be grateful for the contents of your emergency pack.

Although you might moan about it sometimes because you'd rather be doing your own thing, covering other teachers' classes can actually be a positive experience. For one thing, it helps you get to know your way around the school and meet members of staff you don't normally see. You also get to see how other departments run and how kids behave in these different environments. Useful stuff.

Development Work

This can turn into 'envelopment work', so be warned! When it comes to doing something extra, your priority has to be your work in the classroom with the kids. You don't have a filing cabinet full of materials; you're only just starting to make these up, and so every single worksheet you create is a piece of development work. Building up resources, familiarising yourself with texts, getting used to parents' nights, reporting and recording, and the other day-to-day responsibilities of being a teacher (excessive coffee drinking and overuse of rhetorical questions!) are the things you need to concentrate on.

Another aspect of development work is the twilight courses provided by the authority you work for, which will range from mind-numbingly boring to totally inspiring. It's worthwhile checking them out – your school should have a catalogue. In my first year, for example, I remember going to some great courses run by Edinburgh on teaching Higher Literature (and no, they didn't pay me anything extra to say that!).

There are also some things you'll want to plug into at the school. I remember running lunch-time classes twice a week in the second term for my fourth-years so that they could do some extra work on their folios. I also tutored one of our CSYS pupils for her dissertation. My departmental responsibility was to establish a link with one of our associated primaries. The project came to fruition in the summer term, when we carried out a cross-phase primary / secondary lesson sequence at the primary. I also arranged the publicity for our school book week (important lesson learned – you don't need to pick the phone up when using the fax machine!).

I enjoyed doing all of the above, most of which was well suited to my personality and provided the opportunity to develop skills that were ultimately of benefit to me and the kids. You may want to do less in your first year, you may want to do more – the choice is yours. The important thing is not to try to run before you can walk.

In my second year I joined a couple of committees that were of particular interest to me, and I learned a great deal from these, particularly the Language and Learning Steering Group – being a member of that committee really informed my teaching.

It's better to do one thing well than a few things badly. Don't be a 'yes-person' at the expense of your peace of mind. You'll want to be seen as a team player and someone who can pull their weight, but, at the same time, you don't have to do everything in your first year. It would be a shame if you burnt yourself out in an attempt to dazzle people! Human combustion – spontaneous or otherwise – is always a bad idea.

Extra-curricular Activities

When you take part in activities outwith school hours, this says a lot to your pupils about the level of your commitment to them. They really do appreciate this, and you very rarely have to be too 'teacherly' during these activities. Pupils don't generally give up their free time to have a carry on – you normally see them at their best.

It's during the theatre trips or musical rehearsals that relationships with your pupils are forged, and these activities give you a much broader view of the children that you teach. They also, very importantly, let your pupils see that teachers don't live in school cupboards – a revelation to many of them!

It's also well worth your while getting involved in staff social events. Sometimes you'll be exhausted after a hard day, but make the effort – you'll have fun! Staff get-togethers give you the chance to unwind with your colleagues and see the human (sometimes very human!) side of them. It's really weird seeing certain colleagues with their guard down or in casual clothes, but this will probably make them less formidable and a whole lot more interesting and likeable in your eyes. I particularly enjoy getting the chance to have a good chat with the rest of my department – there's surprisingly little time to do this during the school day, and it's nice to have peace to chill with them for a change.

Pupil Management

Of all the things that terrified me about starting my first year of probation, the thing that had me quaking in my boots (well, sandals – it was the summer!) was pupil management. My stream of consciousness went something like this:
- – I hope they like me
- – what if they all ignore me when I ask them to listen?
- – I wish I was taller
- – what if somebody swears at me?
- – what if I've forgotten how to do this over the holidays?
- – what if they're mean to me?

I even dreamed about it. But I'm still going strong 'x' years later (!), although these fears never totally fade (especially about forgetting everything during the holidays). So hang in there – you do develop strategies and you are not alone.

It's worth remembering that teachers are in a constant state of getting to know their pupils. When I started out, my fourth-years were pretty horrible to me because they had had a series of supply teachers the year before, and they thought I was just another adult passing through. Schools can be very territorial,

and when you are new you have to realise that the kids see you as a stranger on their turf. In the beginning I couldn't imagine ever looking forward to seeing that class arrive at my door, but gradually things changed. No magic formula I'm afraid – sometimes it's just a case of getting used to one another. Trust takes time. You just have to hang in there and – hard, hard lesson – try to learn to separate your 'personal' self from your 'professional' self. When pupils make personal comments about you, and they sometimes will, it's not because they really know you personally, it's because they're kids and kids do that sometimes. They can be astonishingly blunt, but that works two ways: sometimes it can hurt, but sometimes the blunderingly sincere, kind, kind words of my pupils have literally taken my breath away. They can be amazingly sweet too, and these are the moments you need to remember when you've had a bad day.

Don't be afraid to seek advice on how to handle difficult situations. This is not a sign of failure. Sometimes it's easier for a colleague to see how to improve a situation, because they're not as emotionally tangled up in it as you are. Make sure you don't isolate yourself in a nightmare relationship with a class or an individual. My PT and other colleagues gave me great advice on how to improve my relationship with my fourth-years, and, by the October break of my first year, they were like a totally different group of pupils. It was like the Von Trapp kids in *The Sound of Music*! I ended up looking forward to having that class and by the time they came to sit their exams, I was like a mother hen. Remember though; these were the same kids who'd given me such a hard time in August.

When your pupils know you are professionally committed to them and you expect them to be committed to themselves, it makes a big difference. You have to create opportunities for your pupils to show you themselves at their best. I'm not quite sure exactly how this happens, but I do think it has a lot to do with commitment and consistency on your part. So don't ever write a class off, and don't ever accept that they have written you off – things change.

Sometimes new teachers make the mistake of either under-reacting or over-reacting when it comes to discipline or praise. That's because, when you're still finding your identity as a teacher, it can take a while to sort out the difference between what you mind, or find acceptable or pleasing, as a person and what you should mind, or be in raptures about, as a teacher. For example, as a person, I don't mind if someone wants to chew gum while they work, but, as a teacher, I do because in my school, as in most, we have a rule about this and it's my responsibility to uphold these rules.

Try to be positive when discussing rules with your classes and display a copy on the wall. Set reasonable and clear parameters and remember that, once you've set these up, it's important to be consistent and fair in enforcing them. Involving your pupils in formulating rules can be effective, although you have to handle this carefully. The secret is to have your agenda ready and make the kids think it is theirs! Try to appear confident in front of them when dealing with misbehaviour, even if you're shaking in your boots / sandals. If problems arise, resist the temptation to either ignore them or to over-react. Remain calm. Breathe. This too shall pass!

Be as consistent as you can and don't say things and then not follow through. For example, if you say, 'The next person to talk when I'm talking will be staying back after class,' make sure that you remember to keep that person back. This means that you need to learn to think before you speak (rich coming from me, I know!) You won't always get the balance right when you first start out – you're learning all the time. Sometimes you'll over-react, other times you'll let kids off with stuff you shouldn't. Time is short, but try to reflect on how you're doing on this.

Difficult Situations

As a probationer, it's vital that you investigate and use the departmental and whole-school mechanisms for dealing both with problematic behaviour and with pupils who are doing very well. You will see that there are usually a clear set of steps that you, as the class teacher, will be expected to take before it becomes appropriate to refer a pupil or a class to your line manager. For example, if a couple of kids are being a nuisance (that word covers a multitude of sins!), the starting point is giving them a warning and, if that doesn't work, splitting them up. If they continue to be a nuisance, try a punishment exercise or a lunch-time detention. For most pupils, a combination of some or all of these measures usually curbs the misbehaviour. It's only if they persist after you have taken all of these steps that you should consider removing one or both of them from the room.

It can be very effective to isolate disruptive pupils by speaking to them in the corridor away from their audience. For a lot of pupils, an appeal to their better nature in the quiet of the hallway works a treat. The golden rule is to keep calm and be reasonable (even when you feel like nobody else is!) and remember that a sense of humour or a sensitive word can work wonders in some potentially explosive situations. However, if these fail, make sure you go on to follow the next step in your school's official policy on pupil management. That usually means a referral to your line manager.

There are rare occasions when a pupil's misbehaviour is so extreme, you need to bypass some of the normal steps in the disciplinary chain. If, for example, a pupil throws a chair at someone or tells you in no uncertain terms where to go, it's generally best to take strong measures straight away, so referring that pupil immediately would obviously be appropriate.

Be aware that referring pupils in this way is not seen by most kids as weakness or admission of failure on your part, but rather it is seen as a positive action, a means of dealing effectively with certain situations. There are some individuals who really need to know that it is not simply you that they are taking on, but that you have a whole line of back-up at your disposal and you are prepared to use it. And it's not just probationers who refer pupils: you'll find that your PT will refer kids to the appropriate AHT and that AHTs refer kids to the Head.

If you have a pupil who is 'trouble' on a regular basis, it can help to plan out strategies for dealing with him/her in advance. I've been known to discuss tactics with my PT before teaching a class containing a certain – how shall I put it? – 'challenging' pupil, so that I know that if he does this, I'll do this and if he does that, I'll do that. I call it the 'game of chess' approach. You don't want to be pessimistic and expect problems where they may not arise, but at the same time it can really help if you are prepared and have had time to think and anticipate certain moves. It's always a great relief if you don't have to use them.

You can also ask colleagues for helpful hints and successful strategies. They may have spent the previous year with that child and, while they may not have the answer, they'll definitely have a useful list of do's and don'ts.

As I said earlier, watch for trouble zones, like the last period in the afternoon, when neither you nor your pupils are at your best. Plan simple, quiet activities for these lessons, not the kind that are going to make the kids even more hyper or have you jumping through hoops. When making decisions about discipline, try to take a step back and make a judgement according to the dynamics of the class, the time of day, and so on, recognising that it is easy to over-react when you are hot and bothered and your feet are sore.

If you've seen an improvement in a pupil's behaviour, effort, or work, or if you have someone in your class who always works hard and behaves, you need to recognise this. Positive reinforcement is vital, but again, unless a pupil has made a drastic improvement, you don't want to start with a note to the Head Teacher. I mean, what are you going to do for an encore – write to the President? (I know we don't have a President, but I thought it sounded more dramatic!) There are a number of possible approaches – verbal praise; positive comments in jotter; a star or a sticker; a credit / merit point; a positive referral; a certificate; a pupil of the week / month award. Corny as it may sound, accentuating the positive may not entirely eliminate the negative, but it will create a more healthy and satisfying working environment for both you and your classes.

Always reward good behaviour and effort if you can. This is particularly important when you are new and trying to establish a positive working relationship with your pupils. Remember that as a teacher you have a chance to influence a person's feelings of self-worth, so if you do get something wrong, you shouldn't be afraid to say you're sorry – a quiet word in the 'wronged' pupil's ear can actually work wonders. In my experience, the pupil then respects you more, not less, suddenly seeing a teacher as 'human' – a strange phenomenon for many kids!

Finally, never underestimate the power of praise. You will have noticed from observing other teachers and from your own experience that often the pupils who behave the worst get the most attention. Don't forget the well-behaved ones. They need to know that you notice and appreciate their good behaviour. This can occasionally spark off good behaviour in kids who misbehave because they seek attention. If they see you give lots of attention and praise to others, it may inspire them to change tactics. If you do have a pupil who is trying to make a fresh start and behave, make sure they know that you know, otherwise they may revert to their old ways where they got lots of individual attention because you were always out in the corridor with them. The basics are: be consistent, be fair, and be positive. Try to deal with good and bad behaviour promptly and proportionately, and remember that proactive is better than reactive.

Peripatetic Ramblings

Peripatetic – AKA very pathetic, or sometimes that's how it feels. Who invented the word in the first place? It's like 'spinster' or 'polystyrene' – just loaded with negative connotations. Words like this crop up in schools from time to time; one that sends shivers down my spine is 'departmental meeting' which sounds to me like 'depart mental meeting', as if you have to take leave of your senses before entering. Perhaps this is what one Depute had in mind when he instructed staff to ensure that pupils left assembly in a 'spaced out' fashion.

To get back to the point, I have just moved into my own classroom. My posters are up, my boxes are unpacked and I've started displaying the kids' work. It's bliss, but last year I taught in six different rooms, and so if you're peripatetic you have my deepest sympathy. I know what it's like. If you've got your own room and you think this section's not for you, I'd advise you to read on regardless – what you have one year or in one school you won't necessarily have in the next!

I suppose, in some ways, being peripatetic isn't that different from being a student, in that you're used to teaching in a number of different rooms and you don't have the key to any of them! But what's different is the timescale– what feels fine for six weeks may not feel so great after six months.

Being peripatetic means you have to be more organised than your colleagues who have a room of their own. Also, you won't really be able to unpack your stuff. Your PT should arrange for you to store your materials somewhere, but it's not like having your own room with your own cupboards and space for your David Duchovny poster. Everything has to be shared and negotiated and you have to be very diplomatic. It sucks being homeless sometimes!

The key to success is careful planning on a daily basis. You need to make sure that all the materials you need for each lesson arrive at the room you'll be teaching in before your kids do, and you also need to ensure that they are kept in a safe place in that room. Always carry a folder with spare paper, pencils and forms (punishment exercises, quiet room referrals, positive referrals). It's also a good idea to have a pack of extension activities so that if your kids get through the work you have for them faster than you'd anticipated, you're not left all flustered, desperately trying to think of something else for them to do. Finally, make sure your copy of your timetable has all your room numbers on it, and make sure you carry it with you so that you always know where you're supposed to be next. You always think you'll remember until you forget! Analyse it carefully – if you have the same classes in the same classrooms on a regular basis, you should be able to establish a pretty good system for storage and retrieval of materials.

Some colleagues, albeit a minority, can be very territorial about their rooms (they're often the ones sporting scary-casual at the in-service days!). I have a friend who was rarely able to use the board in a colleague's room in her first year because there was never any space left on the board, but there was always an instruction not to rub anything off! That meant she had to either photocopy or dictate instructions to her kids, as there was no overhead projector available. What a hassle.

That said, most teachers are very sympathetic to the plight of peripatetic staff and, if asked, will often give you shelf and cupboard space, allow you to leave materials in their room, and even give you wall space for displaying work. Find out if you can use OHPs, in which case you can prepare your acetates at home and don't need to worry about whether there'll be space on this or that board. Most OHPs come on trolleys and most schools have lifts, so they're not too difficult to move around.

Here comes State the Obvious II. Remember that if you move desks and chairs in the course of a lesson, you should get your pupils to return them to their original places at the end – and be exact. Be careful about letting pupils borrow things that don't belong to you, like another teacher's stencils or protractors or even pencils. Clean anything you write off the board and always try to leave the room in the same condition that you found it in (if not better). Always finish your lessons in good time, so that you have time to gather your belongings and move on to the next room without having to rush. Usually three minutes is enough time to clear up, but, if you've had the scissors, tissue paper and glue out, make it five!

Finally, use the fact that you are peripatetic to your advantage. You can get lots of great ideas by looking at the tasks that other teachers put up on their boards, considering how they decorate and arrange their rooms, and seeing where they keep things and how they label them. I always imagine myself as a spy taking photos of wall displays with one of those tiny cameras! I've asked around though, and I am not the only 007 wannabe – I have known friends to sit and actually note down activities they have read on someone else's board, so impressed have they been by their quality. It's half desperation, half initiative, and half 'I would have made a good spy' (I never was any good at fractions).

Paperwork and Other Necessities

Marking

This is like ironing – if you let it pile up, it's an absolute nightmare. Try to keep on top of it; the kids need quick written and oral feedback. If you are really organised, you can have a marking pattern where you mark S1 work on a Monday, S2 on a Tuesday, and so on. I'm rarely that organised – I'll tend to do a lot of marking one night and focus on something else, maybe even *NYPD Blue* or *Buffy* (affectionately known as 'Guffy' in my family!) the next. Find out what works for you.

You also need to check if there's a department or whole-school edit code, where 'sp' means spelling mistake, ^ means a word is missing, and so on. Then make sure your pupils know what the symbols in the edit code mean. Decide what you are assessing and let the kids know. For example, you may focus your attention on the quality of ideas in one piece of writing, and layout in another. It's vital that your pupils know what you're looking for. Encourage them to proof-read and edit their own work. Sometimes you might want them to work with each

other on making improvements before they hand something in.

Finally, be organised with your profiling and record-keeping from the start, but make sure that you keep it at a manageable level. This is all tied up with your planning – you need to decide what, when, how and why in advance. In many schools, a system for this is already in place and you just need to learn how to use it. If in doubt ask, and do bear in mind that those colleagues you wish you could be like, who seem so unflappable and serene, have not always been so composed or competent. They had to learn too!

Report Cards and Parents' Evenings

There's a knack to both. Basically the key is to be professional, positive and prepared, always remembering that your little horror is the centre of somebody else's universe and you're going to be speaking or writing to that somebody. Don't presume that behaviour at school mirrors behaviour at home, because it often doesn't – it's the Jekyll and Hyde syndrome.

First of all, the report cards. Obviously you need to know in advance the kind of information you're going to be expected to record (doh!): National Test results, 5–14 Levels, and prelim grades for example. If you've kept on top of your record keeping, this won't be a problem. In fact this section of the report is pretty straightforward. I tend to follow a pattern whereby I fill in the child's name and class at the top and my name at the bottom – that's the first stage and you don't need to be a genius for it! Then I fill in their levels or grades or results and, after that, there's usually a ticky box section about homework, attitude, effort and behaviour. It's at this point that you see the necessity of keeping a clear homework record! After that, it's the progress and next steps section, where you're writing a paragraph or two about the child, and this is the bit you need to watch. I'd recommend adopting the peanut-butter sandwich approach, where you start and end with something positive and put the development need part in the middle. For most kids, it's quite easy to think of something good to report, but there are some who make that difficult. Have a think – do they turn up to class on time? Great, you can write 'Ben is always punctual'!

If a child regularly misbehaves or doesn't make an effort, you need to report this, but always remember that it's the behaviour you're concerned about, so write 'Tabitha's behaviour can be disruptive' rather than 'Tabitha is disruptive.' See the difference? The first allows for the fact that Tabitha's behaviour can also be something else, so there's hope, whereas the second is like an immutable fact, implying that, in effect, you've written that child off.

Until you get the hang of it, I'd recommend practising on paper before committing your ideas to the official report. You'll soon pick up the code. For instance, 'Cathy has a quick and lively mind and is always ready to share her ideas with the class' means

Cathy can't sit still or shut up for five minutes!

Now on to parents' night. Most schools run an appointments system for parents' evenings and, like all appointments systems, these work well to begin with; but, as the evening progresses, it becomes harder to stick to your schedule because people get held up elsewhere. I never really worry about it – somehow it all works out fine in the end.

Although there are some things you have no control over (the national debt, the calories in chocolate, traffic lights), there are some measures that you can take to ensure you keep pretty close to schedule. First of all, make it clear to the kids before parents' night that you can only speak to their parents for five minutes. On the night, if it looks like you're going to get involved in a lengthy discussion, suggest that the parents you're talking to make an appointment to come to see you at some other time. I've never actually had to do this, but it's an option that's there.

If you've kept somebody waiting, do apologise and don't rush them away – they've waited their turn and deserve your full attention.

If there is a problem, the parents of the child in question should know this well in advance of parents' night because you should have been issuing punishment exercises or detentions, writing homework letters, or filing referrals with Guidance or the year head. Nothing should be a surprise. Most parents want to work with the school, but they can't do this if they don't know the score. Parents will presume that everything's fine unless they hear otherwise. It's not fair to land bad news on them at the end of the year when they can't do anything about it.

Parents deserve to see evidence that you have done your best to work with their child, adopting a number of strategies to try to improve their progress, effort, and behaviour. When you actually meet them, be polite and frame things as positively as you can. Have a clear idea beforehand of the points you want to make in terms of the way ahead. Some people like to have jotters or homework records there with them (as 'defence exhibit A').

Exactly the same thing applies with pupils you're pleased with. Their parents should know about this before parents' evening because they should have seen your comments in their child's jotter and because, for instance, you should have issued positive referrals .

I usually enjoy parents' evenings because I love to match up child to parent. You learn so much from this, and I have to say that the vast majority of parents are friendly and genuinely want to support you in supporting their child. One last thing: don't have anything garlicky for your tea that night, and take some mints and a bottle of water with you – all that talking's thirsty work.

Your GTC Report

We're talking General Teaching Council here, not Good Teacher Certificate – that comes later! This is your responsibility – gulp – so it's up to you to make sure that your line manager has all the relevant documentation from the GTC in plenty of time. At the end of your first year you can look forward to the school filling in a provisional report on you, which is complemented at the end of your second year by a full report examining every aspect of your professional development. Scary, yes, but usually a walk in the park compared to 'The Year of the Crit Lesson', which would make an even scarier film than *Misery*, albeit with some similar themes!

How you are assessed will very much depend on your school's / department's policy on probationers. In some schools, members of the management team, as well as PTs and APTs, will ask to visit your classes and watch you teach. This usually feels like it's going to be a nightmare beforehand, but then turns out to be quite productive. In other schools, your assessment will be less apparent, although it will still be taking place; for instance, your line manager will observe you informally as he / she comes into your room on various 'errands'. He /she will ask you regularly how you are getting on and, believe me, will be able to tell a great deal by how you respond. Try to avoid screaming, loud sobs, excessive rocking and hysterical laughter – a referral to the school psychologist is not a great career move.

At the end of your first year, your PT will pass a report on you to your Head Teacher who will then complete a very similar report and send this to the GTC. Since you need to sign the report before it is sent, you don't have to worry about surprises! The GTC will then get in touch and let you know what happens next.

Final Words

I want to be serious here for a minute (thought I'd better prepare you for the shock!). The major difference between being a student and being a probationer is the shift from short-term responsibility (with a support network of college tutors, mentors, regents, and fellow students) to long-term responsibility (where the support you get is generally more superficial). As a probationer, you see the same classes day in and day out, and it's impossible to produce super-duper materials for each lesson. There have to be a few fish suppers in amongst the caviar!

There never seems to be enough time to do everything you want to do for and with your pupils, and the day-to-day reality of seeing class after class can be a bit wearing at first. But, rest assured, you will get used to the shift in pace, and there are a lot of rewards in being a regular teacher that pass students by. As a student you are a great novelty, but as the class teacher you build up a relationship with your pupils that goes far deeper and lasts much longer.

At all costs, guard and nurture your enthusiasm. Ensure your knowledge stays fresh, not just of your subject area(s), but also of the things the kids are interested in. Never forget the privilege you have both of opening young minds to the world of your specialism and of preparing your pupils for adult life.

As a teacher you have an incredible responsibility for which there are incredible rewards. To be in a position to shape young minds is a gift. It is up to you, however, what you do with that gift. Confucius (or another really smart person) he say:

To learn and not grow weary is wisdom;
to teach and not grow weary is love.